Inhaltsverzeichnis

W0302381

⤓ Die Benutzerhinweise zum Download des Zusatzmaterials und den entsprechenden Zusatzcode finden Sie am Ende des Buches.

Inhaltsverzeichnis digitales Zusatzmaterial

Vorwort

Bei den vorliegenden Stationsarbeiten handelt es sich um eine Arbeitsform, bei der unterschiedliche Lernvoraussetzungen, unterschiedliche Zugänge und Betrachtungsweisen und unterschiedliche Lern- und Arbeitstempos der Schüler[1] Berücksichtigung finden. Die Grundidee ist, den Schülern einzelne Arbeitsstationen anzubieten, an denen sie gleichzeitig selbstständig arbeiten können. Die Reihenfolge des Bearbeitens der Einzelstationen ist dabei ebenso frei wählbar wie das Arbeitstempo und meist auch die Sozialform.

Als dominierende Unterrichtsprinzipien sind bei allen Stationen die Schülerorientierung und Handlungsorientierung aufzuführen. Schülerorientierung bedeutet, dass der Lehrer in den Hintergrund tritt und nicht mehr im Mittelpunkt der Interaktion steht. Er wird zum Beobachter, Berater und Moderator. Seine Aufgabe ist nicht das Strukturieren und Darbieten des Lerngegenstandes in kleinsten Schritten, sondern durch die vorbereiteten Stationen eine Lernatmosphäre zu schaffen, in der Schüler sich Unterrichtsinhalte eigenständig erarbeiten bzw. Lerninhalte festigen und vertiefen können.

Handlungsorientierung bedeutet, dass das angebotene Material und die Arbeitsaufträge für sich selbst sprechen. Der Unterrichtsgegenstand und die zu gewinnenden Erkenntnisse werden nicht durch den Lehrer dargeboten, sondern mit der Auseinandersetzung mit dem Material und die eigene Tätigkeit gewonnen und begriffen.

Ziel der Veröffentlichung ist, wie bereits oben angesprochen, das Anknüpfen an unterschiedliche Lernvoraussetzungen der Schüler. Jeder Einzelne erhält seinen eigenen Zugang zum inhaltlichen Lernstoff. Die jeweiligen Stationen ermöglichen das Lernen mit allen Sinnen bzw. den verschiedenen Eingangskanälen. Dabei werden sowohl visuelle (sehorientierte) als auch haptische (fühlorientierte) sowie intellektuelle Lerntypen angesprochen. An dieser Stelle werden auch gleichermaßen die Bruner'schen Repräsentationsebenen (enaktiv bzw. handelnd, ikonisch bzw. visuell und symbolisch) mit einbezogen. Aus Ergebnissen der Wissenschaft ist bekannt: Je mehr Eingangskanäle angesprochen werden, umso besser und langfristiger wird Wissen gespeichert und damit umso fester verankert. Das vorliegende Arbeitsheft unterstützt in diesem Zusammenhang das Erinnerungsvermögen, das nicht nur an Einzelheiten und Begriffe geknüpft ist, sondern häufig auch an die Lernsituation.

Folgende grammatische Themenkreise werden innerhalb der verschiedenen Stationen behandelt:

- Basics
- The sentence
- Tenses
- Revision

[1] Aufgrund der besseren Lesbarkeit ist in diesem Buch mit Schüler auch immer die Schülerin gemeint. Ebenso verhält es sich mit Lehrer und Lehrerin etc.

Materialaufstellung und Hinweise zu den einzelnen Stationen

Basics

Die Seiten 9 bis 20 sind in entsprechender Anzahl zu kopieren und den Schülern bereitzulegen. Als Möglichkeit zur Selbstkontrolle können Lösungsseiten erstellt werden. Manchmal sind offene Aufgaben mit individuellen Lösungen vorhanden, die im Plenum besprochen werden sollten.

S. 9	Station 1	**Irregular plural forms:** Ein Stift und evtl. ein Textmarker werden benötigt.
S. 10	Station 2	**Collective nouns:** Ein Stift wird benötigt.
S. 11	Station 3	**Uncountable nouns (1):** Ein Stift und das digitale Zusatzmaterial werden benötigt.
S. 12	Station 4	**Uncountable nouns (2):** Ein Stift wird benötigt.
S. 13	Station 5	**Nouns:** Ein Stift wird benötigt.
S. 14	Station 6	**Conjunctions (1):** Ein Stift wird benötigt.
S. 15	Station 7	**Conjunctions (2):** Ein Stift und evtl. ein Textmarker werden benötigt.
S. 16	Station 8	**Prepositions:** Ein Stift wird benötigt.
S. 17	Station 9	**Verbs with prepositions:** Ein Stift wird benötigt.
S. 18	Station 10	**Relative pronouns:** Ein Stift und das digitale Zusatzmaterial werden benötigt.
S. 19	Station 11	***To* + infinitive:** Ein Stift und das digitale Zusatzmaterial werden benötigt.
S. 20	Station 12	**Infinitive with or without *to*:** Ein Stift wird benötigt.

The sentence

Die Seiten 21 bis 27 sind in entsprechender Anzahl zu kopieren und den Schülern bereitzulegen. Als Möglichkeit zur Selbstkontrolle können Lösungsseiten erstellt werden. Manchmal sind offene Aufgaben mit individuellen Lösungen vorhanden, die im Plenum besprochen werden sollten.

S. 21	Station 1	**Inversion:** Ein Stift wird benötigt.
S. 22	Station 2	**Position of prepositions:** Ein Stift wird benötigt.
S. 23	Station 3	**Prepositions in relative clauses:** Ein Stift wird benötigt.
S. 24	Station 4	***If, when* or *unless*?:** Ein Stift wird benötigt.
S. 25	Station 5	**Contact clauses:** Ein Stift und das digitale Zusatzmaterial werden benötigt.
S. 26	Station 6	**Passive in reported speech:** Ein Stift wird benötigt.
S. 27	Station 7	**Personal passive and impersonal passive:** Ein Stift wird benötigt.

Tenses

Die Seiten 28 bis 36 sind in entsprechender Anzahl zu kopieren und den Schülern bereitzulegen. Als Möglichkeit zur Selbstkontrolle können Lösungsseiten erstellt werden. Manchmal sind offene Aufgaben mit individuellen Lösungen vorhanden, die im Plenum besprochen werden sollten.

S. 28	Station 1	**Simple past, past progressive and present perfect:** Ein Stift wird benötigt.
S. 29	Station 2	**Mixed past tenses (1):** Ein Stift und das digitale Zusatzmaterial werden benötigt.
S. 30	Station 3	**Mixed past tenses (2):** Ein Stift und das digitale Zusatzmaterial werden benötigt.
S. 31	Station 4	**Future with *will/going to*:** Ein Stift wird benötigt.
S. 32	Station 5	**Other future forms:** Ein Stift wird benötigt.
S. 33	Station 6	**Mixed future tenses:** Ein Stift wird benötigt.
S. 34	Station 7	**Past participles (1):** Ein Stift wird benötigt.
S. 35	Station 8	**Past participles (2):** Ein Stift und das digitale Zusatzmaterial werden benötigt.
S. 36	Station 9	**The passive with different tenses:** Ein Stift wird benötigt.

Revision

Die Seiten 37 bis 48 sind in entsprechender Anzahl zu kopieren und den Schülern bereitzulegen. Als Möglichkeit zur Selbstkontrolle können Lösungsseiten erstellt werden. Manchmal sind offene Aufgaben mit individuellen Lösungen vorhanden, die im Plenum besprochen werden sollten.

S. 37	Station 1	**Uncountable nouns:** Ein Stift wird benötigt.
S. 38	Station 2	**Conjunctions:** Ein Stift und das digitale Zusatzmaterial werden benötigt.
S. 39	Station 3	***To* + infinitive:** Ein Stift wird benötigt.
S. 40	Station 4	**Infinitive with or without *to*:** Ein Stift wird benötigt.
S. 41	Station 5	**Position of prepositions:** Ein Stift wird benötigt.
S. 42	Station 6	**Simple past, past progressive and present perfect:** Ein Stift wird benötigt.
S. 43	Station 7	**Mixed past tenses (1):** Ein Stift und das digitale Zusatzmaterial werden benötigt.
S. 44	Station 8	**Mixed past tenses (2):** Ein Stift wird benötigt.
S. 45	Station 9	**Future with *will/going to*:** Ein Stift wird benötigt.
S. 46	Station 10	**Mixed future tenses:** Ein Stift wird benötigt.
S. 47	Station 11	**Past participles:** Ein Stift und das digitale Zusatzmaterial werden benötigt.
S. 48	Station 12	**Reported speech and passive:** Ein Stift wird benötigt.

Route Card

for ____

Obligatory stations

Station number	done	checked
number _____		
number _____		
number _____		
number _____		
number _____		
number _____		
number _____		
number _____		
number _____		

Optional stations

Station number	done	checked
number _____		
number _____		
number _____		
number _____		
number _____		

Station 1

Name: ______________________

Irregular plural forms

Task 1

Look at the nouns in these three texts. Underline or highlight those which have either an irregular plural form or no singular form.

1. There's a noticeboard in the entrance of a supermarket where people can offer things for sale.

   One card read:

   > FOR SALE: Ten white mice.
   > Cheap.

   It was still there a week later, but it now read:

   > FOR SALE: Ten white mice.
   > Cheap. 22 mice FREE!

2. Tom emigrated to Canada. One winter he went ice-fishing on a lake. He sat for hours around a hole in the ice without catching a single fish. The woman near him caught fish after fish.
   "Excuse me," he asked. "What's your secret?"
   "Kpwumpfflwum," she replied.
   "I'm sorry. I couldn't understand that," Tom said.
   The woman poured hot coffee into a cup. Then she spit into the cup three times.
   "You've got to keep the worms warm," she said.

3. Mrs Dougal and Mr O'Connor were neighbours. Mrs Dougal kept a few chickens. Mr O'Connor had a poultry farm with dozens of chickens, ducks and turkeys. There was no fence between them and Mr O'Connor's poultry often came over to Mrs Dougal's garden and shared her chickens' feed. One day Mrs Dougal decided that this had to stop, so she sent Mr O'Connor the following e-mail:
   Thank you for allowing your poultry to feed on my property. I enjoy the fresh eggs they leave every day.
   That night she heard sounds of hammering and the next morning she saw that Mr O'Connor had put up a tall wire fence (*Drahtzaun*) around his property.

Task 2

Complete these two lists of the nouns from the texts.

	SINGULAR	IRREGULAR PLURAL	GERMAN
1.	person	people	*Person, Mensch – Leute, Menschen*
2.	______________	mice	______________
3.	fish	______________	______________
4.	woman	______________	______________

NO SINGULAR FORM

5.	ice	*Eis*	6.	______________	______________
7.	______________	______________	8.	______________	______________

Station 2

Collective nouns

Name: ____________

Task

Choose the correct English collective nouns and their German translations from the boxes.

bedlinen	glassware	cutlery
clothes	people	poultry
cattle		
furniture	crockery	stationery

Menschen	Bettwäsche	Besteck
Büromaterial	Geflügel	Geschirr
Kleidung	Möbel	Rindvieh
Glas		

1. men, women, children
= ____________
____

2. chickens, ducks, turkeys
= ____________
____

3. knives, forks, spoons
= ____________
____

4. cups, plates, dishes
= ____________
____

5. sheets, pillowcases
= ____________
____

6. glasses, bottles
= ____________
____

7. notepaper, envelopes
= ____________
____

8. cows, calves, bulls
= ____________
____

9. chair, sofa, cupboard
= ____________
____

10. socks, shirt, trousers
= ____________
____

Name:

Uncountable nouns (1)

Task 1

Read the German text and then fill in the missing words in the English text.

Frau Gibbons hatte einige Kollegen aus ihrer Firma zu einer Party eingeladen. Es gab viel Musik, Essen und Getränke. Dan hatte viel Spaβ. Er tanzte mit zwei hübschen Mädchen und trank viel Mineralwasser. Er aβ einige Sandwiches und viele Kartoffelchips und Erdnüsse. Später trank er ein groβes Glas Rotwein und aβ ein wenig Käse und Brot und etwas Räucherfisch. Dann entdeckte er die Riesentomaten! Sie waren mit einer köstlichen Sahne gefüllt. Es lagen drei dieser gefüllten Tomaten auf dem Tisch und Dan aβ sie alle drei. Am Ende der Party sagte Dan Frau Gibbons, dass ihm alles sehr gefallen habe. Frau Gibbons antwortete etwas spitz: „Ja, ich habe es bemerkt. Sie haben sogar die Dips gegessen!“

Mrs Gibbons had invited some colleagues from her firm to a party. There was plenty of ______________________ 1, ______________________ 2 and drinks. Dan had a good ______________________ 3. He danced with two pretty girls and drank lots of ______________________ 4. He ate a few sandwiches and lots of crisps and peanuts. Later he had a big glass of red ______________________ 5 and a little ______________________ 6 with ______________________ 7 and some smoked ______________________ 8. Then he discovered the giant tomatoes! They were filled with a delicious ______________________ 9. There were three of these filled tomatoes on the table and Dan ate all three! At the end of the party Dan told Mrs Gibbons that he had enjoyed everything. Mrs Gibbons said rather sharply, “Yes, I noticed. You even ate the dips!”

Task 2 “Track 1”

Now listen to the complete English text and check your answers.

The missing nouns from the English text have no plural forms. They are uncountable nouns.

Station 4

Name: ______________________

Uncountable nouns (2)

Task

Fill in the correct amount: *a few, a little, much* or *many*.

1. I played ______________________ music.
2. Our family doesn't eat ______________________ meat.
3. How ______________________ sugar would you like in your tea?
4. How ______________________ sausages would you like?
5. I was hungry, so I ate ______________________ biscuits.
6. I have ______________________ things to do, but only ______________________ time in which to do them!
7. There weren't ______________________ people at the meeting.
8. Tom Sinclair doesn't have ______________________ friends at school.
9. I couldn't sleep, so I drank ______________________ warm milk.
10. Sheila invited ______________________ friends to her new flat for a party.
11. Please hurry up because we don't have ______________________ time left.
12. Barry didn't drive home because he had had ______________________ drinks.
13. How ______________________ money have we saved for our holiday?
14. How ______________________ grandchildren do Mr and Mrs Evans have?
15. We were able to find ______________________ of the information we needed on the Internet.
16. When I dropped the money, ______________________ coins rolled down the drain (*Gulli*).

Nouns

Name: ______________________

Mr Whittaker usually gets up at about nine o'clock on a Saturday morning and, after a hearty breakfast, he walks to the corner of the street where Retep Mahdlo and his family run a general store. The Mahdlos are Asians and they sell just about everything from apples, bacon and coffee through to scissors, tea, underpants, vacuum-cleaner-bags, walking sticks, xerox paper, yachting magazines, and zippers. Mr Whittaker bought a newspaper and walked home. His home was in the middle of a quiet residential street. Before he opened the door of his house, he stopped and talked to the Taylors, the friendly couple who lived next door. There was some mail on the floor under the letterbox which he picked up as he entered. The postcard with the photo of sheep and Highland cattle was from his daughter, who was working as a waitress in Inverness. There was a letter from his son, who was with the army in Germany. There was something from a charity telling him that feeding the hungry was his responsibility and a local-government-pamphlet telling him that saving water was a good citizen's duty. Then he heard his wife's voice. The door of the living room was open and he saw that their new furniture had arrived. Mabel was telling the men from the transport firm where to put it. Mr Whittaker listened with a smile. After they had left, he would probably have to rearrange everything several times anyway. It was always the same. "Well, there goes my lazy afternoon," he thought.

Task 1

List five proper nouns from the text.

____

Task 2

List five uncountable nouns from the text.

____

Task 3

Write the plural forms of these nouns from the text.

1. letterbox ____________________
2. sheep ____________________
3. waitress ____________________
4. charity ____________________
5. wife ____________________
6. man ____________________

Task 4

Find nouns from the text to complete these expressions.

1. five pounds of ____________________
2. a slice of ____________________
3. a cup of ____________________
4. a pair of ____________________
5. a herd of ____________________
6. a piece of ____________________

Station 6

Name: ____________________

Conjunctions (1)

Task 1

Link these common English conjunctions with their German meanings.

1. and	A) *nicht nur … sondern auch*
2. or	B) *sowohl … als auch*
3. but	C) *und auch; ebenso wie*
4. both … and	D) *weder … noch*
5. not only … but also	E) *und*
6. either … or	F) *aber; sondern*
7. neither … nor	G) *oder*
8. as well as	H) *entweder … oder*

1		2		3		4		5		6		7		8	

Task 2

Complete the sentences with one of the conjunctions (1–8) from Task 1.

1. You can go ____________________ stay – I don't care!
2. I've read the text several times, ____________________ I still don't understand it!
3. You can't have both. Choose ____________________ a ham sandwich ____________________ a chicken sandwich.
4. Paul is ____________________ good-looking ____________________ clever. I don't know what Diana sees in him!
5. What that man said was ____________________ wrong, ____________________ very rude!
6. ____________________ Tim ____________________ Emily have passed their driving tests.
7. We've got tea, coffee ____________________ lots of soft drinks. ____________________ would you like something stronger?
8. Her music is like caviar – you ____________________ love it ____________________ hate it!
9. The children were all singing ____________________ laughing ____________________ having a good time.
10. Danny is my best friend ____________________ my cousin.

Station 7

Conjunctions (2)

Name: ______________________

Basics

Task

Read the text and either underline or highlight the conjunctions.

I walked into the room and closed the door. Neither Mr Buckley nor Mr Wood greeted me or looked up. I examined their faces before I sat down, but their expressions were unreadable. I couldn't tell if they were angry or pleased. These two never betray an emotion unless they intend to do so. They make me nervous because I never know what to expect.

Mr Buckley spoke first. "Your sales promotion campaign in the USA was disappointing," he said. "We've asked you here in order to find out what went wrong."

"We have a report from our export department," added Mr Wood. "We'll start with that unless you have something to say first." Although there were many things I wanted to say, I thought it wiser to remain silent for the moment.

"The report is very thorough," began Mr Buckley and paused ominously. Mr Wood continued. "It places the responsibility for the catastrophe firmly on you." He let a sheet of paper fall from his hand onto the table in front of him and sat back. As if this wasn't clear enough, Mr Buckley clarified it for me. "They claim, Ms Turner, that you made some very serious mistakes."

It looks as if I've got a problem, I thought to myself. Even if the report was nonsense, I'd have trouble proving it. I needed time to think. "I can't comment on their report because I haven't been given a copy," I told them. Mr Wood placed a single sheet of paper in front of me. "We'll wait until you've read it before we go on, shall we?" Both picked up their cups and turned away from me to stare out of the window.

Station 8

Name: ______________

Prepositions

Task 1

Translate the following sentences into English. Use a preposition from the box.

along	across	into	out of	past	after	towards	through

1. Ich ging über die Straße. ______________
2. Sie lief dem Bus hinterher. ______________
3. Wir gingen die Straße entlang. ______________
4. Amy ging durch den Park. ______________
5. Ich sah aus dem Fenster. ______________
6. Sie rannten ihrem Freund entgegen. ______________
7. Ich ging in sein Büro. ______________
8. Du gingst an ihm vorbei. ______________

Task 2

Translate the underlined prepositions into German.

1. Susan Cornwall writes novels about a pathologist. ______________
2. We used the branch as a ladder. ______________
3. That picture was painted by my grandmother. ______________
4. We're open every day except Sunday. ______________
5. Tell Mike that I've got something for him. ______________
6. What would you like for lunch? ______________
7. This morning I bought the Sun instead of the Mirror. ______________
8. This is a photo of the camping site in Spain. ______________
9. Dick looks like an idiot in those silly clothes! ______________
10. There were over twenty people in the queue for the bus. ______________
11. George came with his new girlfriend, Sarah. ______________
12. You mustn't travel on the bus without a ticket. ______________

Name: ______________________

Verbs with prepositions

Task 1

Translate the German verbs into English by choosing a verb and a preposition from the boxes.

agree, cut (3x), blow, find, aim, ask, get (2x), cheer, break (2x), climb, drop, give (2x), fall (2x), hand, fill, grow, show, set

off (3x), away, in (2x), at, out (5x), over, up (7x), behind, down, with, for

1. *aufwachsen* ____________ 2. *absägen, fällen* ____________
3. *abschneiden* ____________ 4. *ausschneiden* ____________
5. *zustimmen* ____________ 6. *angeben* ____________
7. *bitten um* ____________ 8. *aufgeben* ____________
9. *ausscheiden* ____________ 10. *einbrechen* ____________
11. *ausbrechen* ____________ 12. *verschenken* ____________
13. *zurückbleiben* ____________ 14. *hinfallen, umfallen* ____________
15. *heraufklettern* ____________ 16. *aussteigen* ____________
17. *ermuntern* ____________ 18. *aufstehen* ____________
19. *sprengen* ____________ 20. *errichten* ____________
21. *ausfüllen* ____________ 22. *verteilen* ____________
23. *(ab)zielen auf* ____________ 24. *herausfinden* ____________

Task 2

Translate these sentences into English.

1. Wo bist du aufgewachsen? ____________
2. Wem gehört diese Tasche? ____________
3. Stimmst du John oder Susan zu? ____________
4. Wo sind die Diebe eingebrochen? ____________

Basics

Station 10

Relative pronouns

Name: ______________________

Task 1 "Track 2"

Listen to the text and fill in the missing relative pronouns.

BLARNEY, ______________________ [1] has versions for both Windows and Macintosh, is a complete text-processing and layout program. It contains formatting options ______________________ [2] can be used by both amateur and professional users. It provides all the features ______________________ [3] experienced users now expect from a competent word processor. There are pull-down menus ______________________ [4] offer easy-to-use options. There is a built-in universal converter ______________________ [5] can open any document ______________________ [6] the program ______________________ [7] created it. The well-organized printed handbook is also available on-screen, ______________________ [8] saves time. Users ______________________ [9] register their software with us will be offered a 50 per cent reduction on all future up-dates. A free download service is also available to all users ______________________ [10] registration number is known to us.

Task 2

Complete the following sentences with one of the relative pronouns from Task 1.

1. A relative pronoun that relates to people and pets with names: ______________________.
2. A relative pronoun that relates to things and animals without names: ______________________.
3. A relative pronoun that relates to people, things and animals: ______________________.
4. A relative pronoun that expresses possession: ______________________.
5. The additional word *-ever* has a generalising function, e.g.

   a) irgendwer = ______________________,

   b) irgendwas = ______________________,

   c) irgendwelche = ______________________.

Station 11

Name: ______________________

To + infinitive

Task 1

The word *to* has been removed from the following text. Read it carefully and mark the places where it is missing. The first one is done for you.

© drhfoto – fotolia.com

I'll never forget Whitley Bay. My parents used to take me there for a holiday in the summer. We would spend one or even two weeks at a drab boarding house in a side street far from the beach. In those days they couldn't afford stay anywhere else.

I'll never forget the name of the landlady, Mrs Thistlethwaite, because as a child I found it difficult pronounce her name without spitting on the floor. She was a grim woman. Breakfast was at exactly eight o'clock and none of her guests dared be either too early or too late. She expected her guests, whatever their age, behave themselves and do exactly what she told them do. Children had be especially clean and quiet – in other words: invisible. She never forgot remind us not play on the stairs or in the labyrinthine corridors of her Victorian residence. There were usually several young children and she watched us constantly. We knew she was just waiting for us do something wrong and then she would complain our parents. Mrs Thistlethwaite made all her guests leave the boarding house by nine o'clock so that their rooms could be cleaned. And she let nobody return until tea-time at five o'clock. And so after a breakfast of weak tea and thin slices of bread and margarine with jam it was time for us enjoy the attractions of Whitley Bay: seaside shops selling candy floss, rock and fish and chips, an amusement park called 'Fun City' and, ultimately, the sea beyond a long sandy beach. I can remember all these things with pleasure.

But rainy days in Whitley Bay were hell. You couldn't sit on the beach for hours in the rain and an icy wind. The cinemas didn't open until the evening and after an hour or so even 'Fun City' failed appeal. I can remember sitting in spartan cafés – they were all the same: uncomfortable chairs and formica table-tops with overflowing ashtrays and puddles of spilled tea or coffee – and trying make a small glass of orange juice last an hour.

I'd love return Whitley Bay, but when I do, it will be on a fine sunny day and I'll keep well away from those gloomy boarding houses of my childhood!

Task 2 ⬇ "Track 3"

Now listen to the complete text and check your answers. The word *to* is missing in sixteen places.

Station 12

Name: ____________________

Infinitive with or without *to*

Task

Read the grammatical summaries in the box below and then complete the following sentences with the verbs in brackets either with or without *to*.

We use the **infinitive without *to***
- after a modal auxiliary,
- after the negation with *don't*,
- after the verb *let*,
- after *would rather*.

We use the ***to*-infinitive**
- after *how, what, where, when, which*,
- after an adjective,
- after a phrase with *for*.

!
After ***help*** and ***known*** we can use the infinitive either with or without *to*.

1. (remember) I can ____________________ the names of all the kids in the street where I was born and grew up.
2. (build) Mary helped me ____________________ a garden shed.
3. (visit) Rome is a wonderful place ____________________.
4. (get to) Can you tell me how ____________________ the town hall, please?
5. (keep) The neighbours let me ____________________ my scooter in their double garage.
6. (have) In Britain I'd rather ____________________ a meal in a pub than in a restaurant.
7. (eat) My sister is a vegetarian: she doesn't ____________________ meat.
8. (finish) We waited for Doris ____________________ her coffee.
9. (stay) Will you ____________________ for lunch?
10. (lose) I've never known her ____________________ her composure.
11. (borrow) My parents sometimes let me ____________________ the car.
12. (look) How embarrassing! I didn't know where ____________________!
13. (go on) We were all too tired ____________________ .

Station 1

Name: ______________________

Inversion

In formal English, adverbials which have a restrictive or negative meaning are used at the beginning of a sentence when we want to emphasize them. Then we change the position of subject and auxiliary verb:
Rarely *have I been asked to make a speech.*
In no way *does this justify the mistake.*
Never *have we laughed so much!*
This change of position of subject and auxiliary is called **inversion**.

Task 1

Link the English and the German adverbial phrases.

1. rarely, seldom
2. no sooner … than
3. not only … but
4. nowhere else
5. in no way
6. under no circumstances

A) *nirgendwo sonst*
B) *nicht nur … sondern auch*
C) *kaum … als/da*
D) *selten, kaum*
E) *unter keinen Umständen, keinesfalls*
F) *auf keinen Fall, in keiner Weise*

1 ☐ 2 ☐ 3 ☐ 4 ☐ 5 ☐ 6 ☐

Task 2

Rewrite the following sentences using inversion. Be careful with subordinate clauses. (Only the main clause is inverted.)

1. We had hardly finished our meal when the phone started ringing.

   Hardly ____

   ____

2. Mrs Thompson had no sooner left one meeting than she had to go to another.

   ____

   ____

3. We realized only then what we had done.

   ____

4. I have seldom met such an unpleasant person.

   ____

The sentence

Name: ____________

Position of prepositions

Task

Where do the prepositions go? Rewrite the sentences with the prepositions in brackets.

1. on, of, in — The atlas is the third shelf the bookcase my room.

2. on, of — Sydney is the south-east coast and it's the capital New South Wales.

3. at, in, at — Your train will arrive platform eight five minutes and will leave 8.55.

4. with, to, near — I often play darts my friends. We go a local pub my home.

5. to, for, at — We often go Italy a short holiday Christmas.

6. at, on, in — Sandra was born 6 a.m. 21st October 1996.

7. in, since — Jim has lived New York 1999.

8. for, until — We had to wait half an hour the post office opened.

Prepositions in relative clauses

Name: ____________________

Task

Read the grammatical explanation and then rewrite the following formal sentences in an informal style.

> The preposition of a verb is usually at the end of the sentence. In formal English the preposition comes before the question word or the relative pronoun.
> informal: *Treadstone is the firm we usually work* ***for****.*
> formal: *Treadstone is the firm* ***for which*** *we usually work.*

1. This isn't something to which we can agree.

   ____

2. This is the street in which my grandparents used to live.

   ____

3. Is this a lie with which you want to live?

   ____

4. Do you know the names of all the stations through which we pass?

   ____

   ____

5. I can't remember the name of the person to whom I was talking.

   ____

   ____

6. This elderly lady was the young girl with whom I used to play.

   ____

   ____

7. My parents still have the bike on which I learned to ride.

   ____

8. Is this the young girl about whom we were talking?

   ____

9. The police searched for the book in which he had hidden the money.

   ____

   ____

10. We looked for something with which we could start a fire.

   ____

Name: ______

If, when or *unless?*

Task

The conjunctions *if*, *when* and *unless* are missing in the following sentences. Rewrite the sentences with the correct conjunction in the correct place.

1. A Mr James might call and he does, make an appointment for next Thursday.
2. I'm expecting an important fax from a client. Please bring it to me it arrives.
3. I'm having a meeting, so don't put through any calls they're very important.
4. We'll take a taxi from the airport we arrive.
5. We'll only take a taxi from the airport we're short of time.
6. We won't take a taxi from the airport we're short of time.
7. She'll call us she arrives at her hotel.
8. He won't call us something goes wrong.
9. We won't buy anything from your firm you can't deliver on time.
10. We won't buy anything from your firm you deliver on time.
11. We'll pay your invoice our branch office confirms delivery.

Name: ____________

Contact clauses

Task 1

Tick the sentences which are contact clauses and cross out *(durchstreichen)* the relative pronoun.

1. The people that I work with aren't very friendly. ☐
2. The young man who applied for the job was completely unsuitable. ☐
3. Does the train that you come to work on stop in Shoreditch? ☐
4. The dog, whose name was Nanny, loved playing with children. ☐
5. 'Guernica' is one of the most famous pictures which Picasso painted at this time. ☐
6. This is a photo which I took on my business trip to Dundee. ☐
7. The quiz show that we watch usually asks some very difficult questions. ☐
8. Someone stole the bike that I left outside the fitness studio. ☐
9. A word processor is a software program that helps you to write and format a text. ☐
10. I once worked with a man whose name was Charger Hodder. ☐
11. The word processor which I use was designed in the USA. ☐
12. Yes, that's the blue van that I saw parked in front of the bank. ☐
13. What have you done with all the money which your grandparents gave you? ☐
14. The last book that she wrote wasn't as successful as her previous ones. ☐
15. 'Night Hawks' is a painting by Edward Hopper which expresses loneliness. ☐
16. The cruise ship, which starts in Miami, stops at ports in Jamaica and Mexico. ☐

Task 2 ⤓ "Track"

Now listen to the contact clauses and check your answers.

Name: ______________________

Passive in reported speech

Task

Change the direct speech into reported speech. Start with: *I was told/asked …*
Be careful with expressions of time.

1. Your report is to be written by next Tuesday.

   ____

   by the following Tuesday.

2. Your office phone numbers are to be changed tomorrow.

   ____

   ____

3. Your car can be repaired by next Friday.

   ____

   ____

4. When must the bill be paid?

   ____

5. Alice, you are to be given a better job.

   ____

6. Mr Dean, your work has to be corrected far too often!

   ____

   ____

7. These orders have to be entered into the computer.

   ____

   ____

8. Everything had to be checked twice.

   ____

9. The post was delivered an hour ago.

   ____

10. Jane has had a little accident.

    ____

Station 7

Personal passive and impersonal passive

Name: ______________________

The passive form of verbs with two objects

In the active sentence, certain verbs (e. g. *give, offer, tell, promise, send, show*) are followed by two objects: *Her secretary offered me a cup of tea.*

The indirect object (here: *me*) is often a person; the direct object (here: *a cup of tea*) is often a thing.

As a consequence, there are also two passive forms:

- **personal passive:** *I was offered a cup of tea.*
- **impersonal passive:** *A cup of tea was offered to me.*

Task 1

Translate these sentences into English. Use the personal passive and the tenses in brackets.

1. Mir wurde eine bessere Stelle angeboten. (simple past)

   ____

2. Uns wurden Eintrittskarten für das Fußballspiel geschenkt. (present perfect)

   ____

3. Dir waren 100 Dollar versprochen worden. (past perfect)

   ____

4. Ihnen wird schnell die Tür gezeigt werden. (*will*-future)

   ____

Task 2

Change the active sentences to a) the personal passive and b) the impersonal passive.

1. We offered the girls a lift into town.

   a) ____

   b) ____

2. They gave everybody a prize.

   a) ____

   b) ____

3. Mr Miller showed the visitors a film.

   a) ____

   b) ____

The sentence

Station 1

Simple past, past progressive and present perfect

Name: ______________________

Task

Fill in the table without referring to a dictionary or a list of irregular verbs.

	Infinitive	Simple Past	Present Perfect has/have …	Past Progressive was/were …
1.	swim schwimmen	swam	swum	swimming
2.	run			
3.	sit			
4.	make			
5.	take			
6.	dig			
7.	light			
8.	sink			
9.	think			
10.	throw			
11.	feed			
12.	catch			
13.	steal			
14.	lose			
15.	pay			
16.	choose			
17.	ride			
18.	teach			
19.	grow			
20.	meet			

Station 2

Name: ______

Mixed past tenses (1)

Task 1

Complete the text with the words in the brackets. Use the correct past tense forms.

© hardyuno - stock.adobe.com

© matthew clutton / EyeEm - stock.adobe.com

Dr Dillon and his wife (often / visit) ______ 1 Europe. They (take) ______ 2 their holidays in Europe for 15 years now. In all this time they (tour) ______ 3 several countries: Britain, France, Italy, Spain, Germany and Austria. But until last year they (never / stay) ______ 4 in any country longer than a couple of days.

Last summer they (spend) ______ 5 their entire summer holiday in Britain. And they (not stay) ______ 6 in London this time, either. They (choose) ______ 7 a comfortable hotel in Dover, (hire) ______ 8 a car and (drive) ______ 9 along the south coast of England. They (look for) ______ 10 a typical English cottage in a quiet, peaceful village. The Dillons (both / retire) ______ 11 at the beginning of that year. They (live) ______ 12 in a city-centre apartment in Detroit for over 30 years. They (decide) ______ 13 that it (be) ______ 14 time for a change. They finally (find) ______ 15 the place they (look for) ______ 16 in a little village called Polperro.

They (buy) ______ 17 an old fisherman's cottage there which they (modernize) ______ 18.

Task 2 "Track 1"

Now listen to the complete text and check your answers.

Tenses

Station 3

Name: ____________

Mixed past tenses (2)

Task 1

Read the complete text of Station 2 carefully and identify the tenses. Fill in the following table. The first one is done for you.

NO.	SIMPLE PAST	PAST PROGRESSIVE	PRESENT PERFECT	PRESENT PERFECT PROGRESSIVE	PAST PERFECT	PAST PERFECT PROGRESSIVE
1.			✓			
2.						
3.						
4.						
5.						
6.						
7.						
8.						
9.						
10.						
11.						
12.						
13.						
14.						
15.						
16.						
17.						
18.						

Task 2 ⤓ "Track 2"

Listen to the text in Station 2 again. Then look at the answers below and complete the questions.

1. How long ____?
   – The Dillons have been taking their holidays in Europe for the last 15 years.

2. Which ____?
   – They've toured Britain, France, Italy, Spain, Germany and Austria.

3. Where ____?
   – Last summer they spent their holidays in Britain.

4. What ____?
   – They were looking for a typical English cottage in a quiet, peaceful village.

5. Where ____?
   – In Detroit they had been living in a city-centre apartment.

Station 4

Name: ______________________

Future with *will/going to*

It depends on the speaker's intention whether he uses the *will*-future or the *going-to* future.

I'll call home.	*(= spontane Entscheidung/Äußerung)*
I'm going to call home.	*(= überlegter Entschluss)*
Tom will lend me the money.	*(= Vermutung)*
Tom is going to lend me the money.	*(= festes Vorhaben/Abmachung)*
It will rain tonight.	*(= Vermutung, Vorhersage)*
It's going to rain tonight.	*(= kausale Schlussfolgerung)*

If we cannot tell the speaker's intention, we can use either future form.

Task

Read the grammar explanation above. Which future form (*will* or *going to*) is the most suitable future form in these situations?

1. I haven't got a car. – That's OK. ______________________ (I/give) you a lift.
2. I talked to Ian earlier and ______________________ (he/give) us a lift.
3. This new program is terrific! Come on, ______________________ (I/show) you.
4. It's cold in here! – Yes, it is. ______________________ (I/turn) the heating up.
5. I'm expecting a visitor later. So ______________________ (I/turn) the heating up soon.
6. I'm in the middle of cutting the hedges and it's more work than I thought.

   – ______________________ (you/help) me?
7. Dan, your father asked for your help. ______________________ (you/help) him?
8. I'm going out for an hour or two. ______________________ (I/bring back) two pizzas.
9. My parents are going shopping for clothes tomorrow. Dad ______________________ (finally/buy) a new suit!
10. When is Doris coming? – I don't know. ______________________ (I/call) her and ask.
11. I don't know when Alice is coming, so ______________________ (I/call) her this afternoon and ask.

Tenses

Name: ____________

Other future forms

We can use certain expressions to talk about future events:

- Verbs like ***hope to, expect to, want to, would like to,*** etc. are used to say what we think or feel about the future:
  We hope to visit the USA next year.
  We expect to win the cup this year.
- The construction ***am/is/are + to*-infinitive** is quite formal; it is used when something is officially arranged. It often occurs in news reports and official announcements:
  The Duke and Duchess of Kent are to visit Japan next month.

Task

Complete these translations with one of the above expressions. The verbs in the box below can help you.

expect to | report to | hope to | open | want to | make (a speech)

1. Ich erwarte, ihn bald zu sehen.

___

2. Wir wollen nächste Woche ein neues Auto kaufen.

___

3. Sie sollen sich in einer Stunde bei Herrn Madsen melden.

___

4. Der Präsident wird heute Abend eine Rede im Fernsehen halten.

___

___

5. Ich hoffe, morgen angeln gehen zu können.

___

6. Der König wird morgen die Handelsmesse eröffnen.

___

___

Station 6

Name: ______________________

Mixed future tenses

Task 1

Match the tenses in the box below (A–G) with the example sentences (1–7).

A)	future perfect	(*will* + *have* + past participle)
B)	future progressive	(*will* + *be* + *ing*-form)
C)	future perfect progressive	(*will* + *have been* + *ing*-form)
D)	*going to*-future	(*am/is/are going to* + infinitive)
E)	present progressive	(*am/is/are* + *ing*-form)
F)	simple present	(base form of the verb)
G)	*will*-future	(*will* + infinitive)

1. The bus gets into Edinburgh at around eight thirty this evening. ☐
2. You're going to have lots of kids. ☐
3. Don't worry. They won't have heard of you! ☐
4. I'm tired. Will you drive the rest of the way? ☐
5. They're flying to Brazil for a short holiday next week. ☐
6. At ten past three we'll have been waiting here for five hours! ☐
7. Will we also be doing the same thing next week? ☐

Task 2

Complete these sentences with the future perfect form of the verbs.

1. I ______________________ (finish) it by the time you return.
2. Sally ______________________ (talk to) her parents by now.
3. I expect you ______________________ (hear) from him by Friday.
4. The concert ______________________ (not start) yet.
5. Hurry up! Our train ______________________ (not leave) yet.
6. Jane ______________________ (not read) the newspaper yet.
7. ______________________ (they/finish) their meal when we get there?
8. ______________________ (the police/find) the car yet?
9. I think you ______________________ (have) a reply by the weekend.

Tenses

Name: ____________________

Past participles (1)

Task

Fill in the past participle forms of the verbs in the clues.

Across

3. bite
5. become
6. fall
7. draw
9. begin
10. feel
11. bring
14. fly
15. cost
16. drive
18. forget
19. buy
20. do

Down

1. cut
2. freeze
3. bet
4. eat
5. beat
7. dream
8. find
9. break
11. build
12. fight
13. drink
17. come

Station 8

Past participles (2)

Name: ____________________

Task 1 “Track 3”

Listen carefully and fill in the verbs that you hear.

1. ____________________ ____________________
2. ____________________ ____________________
3. ____________________ ____________________
4. ____________________ ____________________
5. ____________________ ____________________
6. ____________________ ____________________
7. ____________________ ____________________
8. ____________________ ____________________
9. ____________________ ____________________
10. ____________________ ____________________
11. ____________________ ____________________
12. ____________________ ____________________
13. ____________________ ____________________
14. ____________________ ____________________
15. ____________________ ____________________
16. ____________________ ____________________
17. ____________________ ____________________
18. ____________________ ____________________
19. ____________________ ____________________
20. ____________________ ____________________
21. ____________________ ____________________
22. ____________________ ____________________

Task 2

Now fill in the past participle forms of the verbs.

Name: ____________

The passive with different tenses

Formation of passive forms

	Tense	Form of Be	Past Participle
A)	infinitive	am/is/are to be	found
B)	modal auxiliary	must be	told
C)	simple present	am/is/are	made
D)	present progressive	am/is/are being	taken
E)	simple past	was/were	hidden
F)	past progressive	was/were being	talked about
G)	present perfect	has/have been	washed
H)	past perfect	had been	said
I)	*will*-future	will be	eaten
J)	*going to*-future	am/is/are going to be	sold

Task

Study the overview above. Then identify the passive forms in the following sentences.

A guided tour

1. We're being shown around the new company headquarters building. ☐
2. So now we all know how and why it was built. ☐
3. We are informed about the aesthetic aims of the architect. ☐
4. and where other examples of her work can be seen. ☐
5. But photos haven't been included in the tour. ☐
6. That's because the floor space in them wasn't being rented. ☐
7. A model of the building is to be found in the executive restaurant, ☐
8. which we are now going to be taken to. ☐
9. They'll probably give us the sandwiches which weren't eaten at lunch. ☐
10. The guide doesn't want to admit that they've all been demolished. ☐
11. It's worse. The sandwiches look as if they had been made the day before! ☐
12. Next we will be shown a film and then we can all go home. ☐

Uncountable nouns

Name: ______________________

Task 1

Which nouns from the box fit the phrases below? Some nouns fit more than one phrase.

bacon beer butter chocolate information milk sauce bread cake cheese coffee lemonade soap tea chocolates (Pralinen) news jeans tuna fish cream soup mustard (Senf) mincemeat (Hackfleisch) sugar pyjamas yoghurt vinegar (Essig) trousers

1.  a can of ______________________
2. a tin of ______________________ 
3.  a jar of ______________________
4. a pound of ______________________ 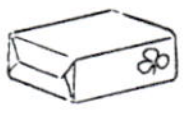
5.  a slice of ______________________
6. an item of ______________________ 
7.  a bottle of ______________________
8. a cup of ______________________ 
9.  a pair of ______________________
10. a packet of ______________________ 

11.  a bar of ______________________
12. a bowl of ______________________ 
13.  a carton of ______________________
14. a box of ______________________ 

Task 2

Complete these translations.

1. *Ich liebe Schokolade.* ______________________
2. *Ich mag Pralinen lieber.* ______________________
3. *Die Polizei ist hier.* ______________________
4. *Ich brauche mehr Informationen.* ______________________

Revision

Station 2

Conjunctions

Name: ______________________

Task 1

Complete the sentences with a conjunction from the box below.

after	if	as if	because of	(in order) to
	although	that	because	

1. ______________________ his qualifications were good, he couldn't find a job.
2. The employees asked their company to change the dress code

   ______________________ they thought it was unfair.
3. The club reduced the membership fee ______________________ many people had complained it was too high.
4. People are spending less ______________________ the poor economic situation.
5. Look at those clouds! It looks ______________________ it's going to rain.
6. I know ______________________ the envelope was addressed to you.
7. ______________________ you're hungry, let me know and I'll make lunch.
8. We stopped at a motorway restaurant ______________________ have a meal and a rest.

Task 2 "Track 1"

Listen to the text and tick (✓) the conjunctions that you hear.

1. after	2. although	3. and	
4. as	5. as well as	6. because	7. both … and
8. because of	9. but	10. if	11. (in order) to
12. even if	13. that	14. unless	

Station 3

To + infinitive

Name:

Task

Complete the sentences with the infinitive forms of a suitable verb from the word square.

Z	F	H	U	M	G	N	N	U	C	B	N	T	E	T
I	A	I	W	C	P	M	P	F	P	X	O	Y	E	A
P	K	R	N	Q	V	B	K	L	L	F	Y	W	J	N
Y	H	D	M	I	O	M	B	E	A	I	I	M	N	G
R	E	W	E	Y	S	L	H	R	Y	N	W	K	E	W
B	V	E	F	W	J	H	A	R	B	D	A	N	G	T
L	S	A	X	A	Q	L	A	T	U	W	J	P	F	B
Y	T	I	Y	D	N	E	Q	O	D	O	P	C	O	U
P	T	S	U	M	W	S	V	N	S	G	Q	R	R	S
D	Y	I	H	K	Q	A	W	Q	A	W	Z	O	D	G
E	Z	P	R	V	V	D	R	E	S	H	I	E	M	=
L	L	M	E	D	T	M	V	W	R	O	E	M	A	W
C	A	B	A	V	J	W	G	B	X	W	L	Q	K	B
K	Q	G	D	S	M	E	E	T	P	I	R	V	E	T
I	L	W	V	F	X	L	Y	O	K	U	Q	Y	E	G

1. We won't go out right now. We'll wait for you ____________________ your meal.
2. I'm sorry, but Mr Wallis is too busy ____________________ you right now.
3. My doctor's handwriting is very difficult ____________________!
4. Excuse me. Can you tell me how ____________________ Conference Room 3, please?
5. She just isn't good enough ____________________ the lead singer in the group.
6. I know how ____________________ quadratic equations.
7. Susan still isn't sure which dress ____________________ for the wedding!
8. My Italian girlfriend showed me how ____________________ lasagne.
9. An accordion isn't the easiest instrument ____________________.
10. Good morning, Ms Lewis. I'm very pleased ____________________ you.
11. Many of the questions in the test were very hard ____________________.

Revision

Name: ____________________

Infinitive with or without *to*

Task

Complete the sentences either with or without *to* and the verbs in brackets.

1. (crawl) Tom felt the huge hairy spider ____________________ over his hand.
2. (crawl) Tom didn't want the spider ____________________ over his hand.
3. (buy) I know where ____________________ the best clothes.
4. (buy) We can't afford ____________________ a new car this year.
5. (need) You'll probably ____________________ your umbrella today.
6. (need) You'll probably ____________________ use your umbrella today.
7. (check) I stopped ____________________ the tyre pressures.
8. (check) I stopped, but I didn't ____________________ the oil.
9. (dance) Sandra likes ____________________, but she won't ____________________ foxtrots and waltzes.
10. (watch) We stood on the cliffs ____________________ the sea.
11. (watch) We often stand on the cliffs and ____________________ the sea.
12. (do) What do we ____________________ in an emergency?
13. (do) Do you all know what ____________________ in an emergency?
14. (stand up) I ran over to the girl and helped her ____________________.
15. (bury) We saw a man ____________________ something in the woods.
16. (bury) He tried ____________________ something in the woods.
17. (make) The Rockefellers knew how ____________________ money!
18. (make) Don't let anyone ____________________ a big fuss about it.
19. (listen to) I think we'd better ____________________ the text again.
20. (listen to) It's important for fishermen ____________________ the weather forecast.

Station 5

Name: ______

Position of prepositions

Frequency:	often always regularly never sometimes usually
Place:	on at opposite over in front of in under between behind
Time:	at after before on since until during in from … to for

Task

Rewrite the sentences with suitable prepositions from the box above.

1. *(vor, um, am)* Let's meet the station 3:30 Saturday afternoon.

2. *(am, während)* Wednesday I went to the bank my lunch break.

3. *(manchmal, am)* I go shopping the weekend.

4. *(immer, von … bis)* The swimming pool is open May September.

5. *(oft, nach)* I hang out with my friends school.

6. *(seit)* Dad and his friends have been playing poker twelve years.

7. *(nie, bis)* The opera is over the tall lady sings.

8. *(gegenüber, in)* The library is the town hall the city centre.

9. *(seit)* We've been sitting here 9:15 this morning!

10. *(gewöhnlich, vor)* I read a book I go to bed.

Simple past, past progressive and present perfect

Name: ______________________

Task 1

Simple past or past progressive? Complete these sentences with the correct past forms of the verbs in brackets.

1. We ______________________ (feel) tired when the coach finally ______________________ (arrive) at our hotel.
2. Colin ______________________ (sit) right next to me when the concert ______________________ (start).
3. We ______________________ (walk) past the art gallery when the accident ______________________ (happen).
4. I ______________________ (wake up) suddenly. The window ______________________ (be) open and it ______________________ (rain).
5. As soon as I ______________________ (hear) the car, I ______________________ (open) the door and ______________________ (run out).
6. As usual they ______________________ (have) a meal and ______________________ (watch) TV when I ______________________ (call).

Task 2

Use the words to make either a statement or a question. Use the simple past or the present perfect.

1. I – drive a car – never

____

2. you – visit Rome – when – be in Italy – last summer?

____

____

3. I – just – buy – a moped

____

4. you – find – your coat – yet?

____

5. anybody – meet Mrs Bell – at her hotel this morning?

____

____

Station 7

Mixed past tenses (1)

Name: ______________________

Task 1 "Track 2"

Listen to the text. Then listen again and fill in the missing verb forms.

Christine ______________________ [1] a new car last month, but she ______________________ [2] her old car yet. She ______________________ [3] her old car to her younger brother Danny for a year. He finally ______________________ [4] his driving test last week. He ______________________ [5] almost forty driving lessons before he ______________________ [6] the test. He ______________________ [7] his first driving test because the examiner ______________________ [8] he ______________________ [9] in the mirror often enough. That ______________________ [10] sometime last April. Christine ______________________ [11] for six years now and she ______________________ [12] any serious accidents. She ______________________ [13] her own car since she ______________________ [14] nineteen.

Task 2

Complete the dialogue with the words in the brackets. Use the correct verb forms.

Sheila: Hello, Carol. (you/talk to) ______________________ [1] Dave Chambers yet?

Carol: Yes, we (have) ______________________ [2] a meeting yesterday afternoon. We (decide) ______________________ [3] to visit the next trade fair in Shanghai.

Sheila: Yes, Dave (tell) ______________________ [4] me about it and I (find) ______________________ [5] useful information about the trade fair on the Internet.

Carol: Good. (you/print) ______________________ [6] it out yet?

Sheila: Not yet. I'm afraid our computer (crash) ______________________ [7] again. We (have) ______________________ [8] problems with the damn thing all this week.

Revision

Station 8

Name: ______________________

Mixed past tenses (2)

Task

Complete the text with the words in brackets. Use the correct past tense of the verbs.

Inspector Boston and Sergeant Lazenby (walk) ______________________ [1] through the jungle for three hours when they (find) ______________________ [2] the body. They (hear) ______________________ [3] the crows and (leave) ______________________ [4] the path to investigate. They (make) ______________________ [5] lots of noise and the angry crows (fly) ______________________ [6] away noisily. And then they (see) ______________________ [7] what they (eat) ______________________ [8].

Inspector Boston (wave) ______________________ [9] away the flies with one hand and (hold) ______________________ [10] a handkerchief to his nose with the other as he (examine) ______________________ [11] the body carefully.

Sergeant Lazenby (switch off) ______________________ [12] her radio. "I'm afraid that I (not/be able to) ______________________ [13] reach our base camp, sir."

"That's a pity," said Boston, "because we're in great danger and we need their help. Whoever (do) ______________________ [14] this (watch) ______________________ [15] us since we (leave) ______________________ [16] our base camp this morning. They (know) ______________________ [17] somebody would come to investigate."

Sergeant Lazenby (search) ______________________ [18] through her backpack.

"Here. You'd better have this." She (throw) ______________________ [19] something heavy towards Boston. He (catch) ______________________ [20] it with one hand. It (be) ______________________ [21] a very deadly-looking automatic pistol.

Station 9

Name: ____________

Future with *will/going to*

Task

Translate these sentences into English. With some sentences the *will*-future is the most suitable, with others the *going to*-future is the most suitable and with some sentences you can use either future form.

1. Der Junge wird gleich vom Fahrrad fallen!

   ____

2. Sei vorsichtig oder du wirst dich verletzen!

   ____

3. Es wird in einer Stunde dunkel.

   ____

4. Ich bin sicher, dass Tom dort sein wird.

   ____

5. Es wird morgen schneien.

   ____

6. Wir werden morgen sehr beschäftigt sein.

   ____

7. Ich habe Hunger, also werde ich mir ein großes Sandwich machen.

   ____

   ____

8. Jane wird das Essen für unsere Party kaufen.

   ____

9. Wir werden an der nächsten Tankstelle halten.

   ____________________________________ filling station.

10. Ich bin sicher, dass Mark diese CD mögen wird.

   ____

Revision

Station 10

Name: ______________

Mixed future tenses

Task

Complete these sentences with the words in brackets. Use a suitable future form of the verbs. Sometimes there is more than one suitable form.

1. Would you like to go out tonight?

   – I can't, ______________________________ (I / study) for an exam.

2. We're absolutely certain that our son ______________________________ (go) to university.

3. The taxi is slowing down. I think ______________________________ (it / stop).

4. By next July my father ______________________________ (work) there for 30 years.

5. What ______________________________ (you / do) at this time tomorrow?

6. If the hotel is full, where ______________________________ (we / stay)?

7. Your room is untidy! – OK. ______________________________ (I / it / tidy up) in a minute or two.

8. We're late. When we finally get there, the concert ______________________________ (finish).

9. Hurry up or when we get to the party, they ______________________________ (eat) all the food on the buffet!

10. I've talked to Barbara and ______________________________ (she / help) us with the computer.

11. What subject ______________________________ (you / talk about) when you give your speech this evening?

Station 11

Name: ______________________

Past participles

Task 1 "Track 3"

Listen carefully and fill in the verbs that you hear.

1. ______________________ ______________________
2. ______________________ ______________________
3. ______________________ ______________________
4. ______________________ ______________________
5. ______________________ ______________________
6. ______________________ ______________________
7. ______________________ ______________________
8. ______________________ ______________________
9. ______________________ ______________________
10. ______________________ ______________________
11. ______________________ ______________________
12. ______________________ ______________________
13. ______________________ ______________________
14. ______________________ ______________________
15. ______________________ ______________________
16. ______________________ ______________________
17. ______________________ ______________________
18. ______________________ ______________________
19. ______________________ ______________________
20. ______________________ ______________________
21. ______________________ ______________________
22. ______________________ ______________________
23. ______________________ ______________________
24. ______________________ ______________________

Task 2

Now fill in the past participle forms of the verbs.

Station 12

Name: ______________

Reported speech and passive

Task 1

Rewrite these sentences in reported speech. Note that the reporting verb is in the past tense.

1. *Tom:* Our next game will be played on the computer.

2. *Detective Wright:* Everybody in the building has been interviewed.

3. *Mr Hall:* It's cold. Have you all been given extra blankets?

4. *Susan:* I heard the news. Have the thieves been caught?

5. *Wendy:* Stop the game before somebody gets hurt!

Task 2

Change these sentences from active to passive.

1. Someone from the office will meet Mr Hirohito at the airport.

2. I have ordered a taxi for Mr Wells.

3. Birds usually build their nests in the spring.

4. Have you informed your parents about the class trip?

5. People think I'm very strange.

6. Where can I find Mr Simpson?

Station 1: Irregular plural forms — page 9

Task 1

1. people, mice
2. ice, fish, woman, coffee
3. poultry, feed

Task 2

2. mouse, *Maus – Mäuse*
3. fish, *Fisch – Fische*
4. women, *Frau – Frauen*
6. coffee, *Kaffee*
7. poultry, *Geflügel*
8. feed, *Futter*

Station 2: Collective nouns — page 10

Task

1. people – *Menschen*
2. poultry – *Geflügel*
3. cutlery – *Besteck*
4. crockery – *Geschirr*
5. bedlinen – *Bettwäsche*
6. glassware – *Glas*
7. stationery – *Büromaterial*
8. cattle – *Rindvieh*
9. furniture – *Möbel*
10. clothes – *Kleidung*

Station 3: Uncountable nouns (1) — page 11

Task 1 and 2

1. music
2. food
3. time
4. mineral water
5. wine
6. cheese
7. bread
8. fish
9. cream

Station 4: Uncountable nouns (2) — page 12

Task

1. a little
2. much
3. much
4. many
5. a few
6. many, a little
7. many
8. many
9. a little
10. a few
11. much
12. a few
13. much
14. many
15. much
16. a few

Station 5: Nouns — page 13

Task 1
Whittaker, Retep Mahdlo/the Mahdlos, the Taylors, Inverness, Mabel (Highland, xerox)

Task 2
bacon, coffee, tea, xerox paper, mail (water, furniture)

Task 3
1. letterboxes
2. sheep
3. waitresses
4. charities
5. wives
6. men

Task 4
1. apples
2. bacon
3. tea/coffee
4. scissors/underpants
5. sheep/cattle
6. furniture

Station 6: Conjunctions (1)

page 14

Task 1

1. E
2. G
3. F
4. B
5. A
6. H
7. D
8. C

Task 2

1. or
2. but
3. either … or
4. neither … nor
5. not only … but also
6. Both … and
7. and, Or
8. either … or
9. and, and
10. as well as

Station 7: Conjunctions (2)

page 15

Task

I walked into the room and closed the door. Neither Mr Buckley nor Mr Wood greeted me or looked up. I examined their faces before I sat down, but their expressions were unreadable. I couldn't tell if they were angry or pleased. These two never betray an emotion unless they intend to do so. They make me nervous because I never know what to expect.

Mr Buckley spoke first. "Your sales promotion campaign in the USA was disappointing," he said. "We've asked you here in order to find out what went wrong."

"We have a report from our export department," added Mr Wood. We'll start with that unless you have something to say first." Although there were many things I wanted to say, I thought it wiser to remain silent for the moment.

"The report is very thorough," began Mr Buckley and paused ominously. Mr Wood continued. "It places the responsibility for the catastrophe firmly on you." He let a sheet of paper fall from his hand onto the table in front of him and sat back. As if this wasn't clear enough, Mr Buckley clarified it for me. "They claim, Ms Turner, that you made some very serious mistakes."

It looks as if I've got a problem, I thought to myself. Even if the report was nonsense, I'd have trouble proving it. I needed time to* think. "I can't comment on their report because I haven't been given a copy," I told them. Mr Wood placed a single sheet of paper in front of me. "We'll wait until you've read it before we go on, shall we?" Both picked up their cups and turned away from me to* stare out of the window.

* (in order) to

Station 8: Prepositions

page 16

Task 1

1. I walked across the street.
2. She ran after the bus.
3. We walked along the street.
4. Amy walked through the park.
5. I looked out of the window.
6. They ran towards their friend.
7. I went into his office.
8. You walked past him.

Task 2

1. *über*
2. *als*
3. *von*
4. *außer*
5. *für*
6. *zum*
7. *statt*
8. *von*
9. *wie*
10. *über*
11. *mit*
12. *ohne*

Station 9: Verbs with prepositions

page 17

Task 1

1. grow up
2. cut down
3. cut off
4. cut out
5. agree with
6. show off
7. ask for
8. give up
9. drop out
10. break in
11. break out
12. give away
13. fall behind
14. fall over
15. climb up
16. get off
17. cheer up
18. get up
19. blow up
20. set up
21. fill in
22. hand out
23. aim at
24. find out

Task 2

1. Where did you grow up?
2. Who does this bag belong to? (To whom does this bag belong?)
3. Do you agree with John or with Susan?
4. Where did the thieves break in?

Station 10: Relative pronouns

page 18

Task 1

1. which
2. which
3. that
4. that
5. which
6. whatever
7. that
8. which
9. who
10. whose

Task 2

1. who
2. which
3. that
4. whose
5. a) whoever, b) whatever, c) whichever

Station 11: *To* + infinitive

page 19

Task 1 and 2

I'll never forget Whitley Bay. My parents used to take me there for a holiday in the summer. We would spend one or even two weeks at a drab boarding house in a side street far from the beach. In those days they couldn't afford to stay anywhere else.

I'll never forget the name of the landlady, Mrs Thistlethwaite, because as a child I found it difficult to pronounce her name without spitting on the floor. She was a grim woman. Breakfast was at exactly eight o'clock and none of her guests dared to be either too early or too late. She expected her guests, whatever their age, to behave themselves and do exactly what she told them to do. Children had to be especially clean and quiet – in other words: invisible. She never forgot to remind us not to play on the stairs or in the labyrinthine corridors of her Victorian residence. There were usually several young children and she watched us constantly. We knew she was just waiting for us to do something wrong and then she would complain to our parents.

Mrs Thistlethwaite made all her guests leave the boarding house by nine o'clock so that their rooms could be cleaned. And she let nobody return until tea-time at five o'clock. And so after a breakfast of weak tea and thin slices of bread and margarine with jam it was time for us to enjoy the attractions of Whitley Bay: seaside shops selling candy floss, rock and fish and chips, an amusement park called 'Fun City' and, ultimately, the sea beyond a long sandy beach. I can remember all these things with pleasure.

But rainy days in Whitley Bay were hell. You couldn't sit on the beach for hours in the rain and an icy wind. The cinemas didn't open until the evening and after an hour or so even 'Fun City' failed to appeal. I can remember sitting in spartan cafés – they were all the same: uncomfortable chairs and formica table-tops with overflowing ashtrays and puddles of spilled tea or coffee – and trying to make a small glass of orange juice last an hour.

I'd love to return to Whitley Bay, but when I do, it will be on a fine sunny day and I'll keep well away from those gloomy boarding houses of my childhood!

Station 12: Infinitive with or without *to*

page 20

Task

1. remember
2. (to) build
3. to visit
4. to get to
5. keep
6. have
7. eat
8. to finish
9. stay
10. (to) lose
11. borrow
12. to look
13. to go on

Station 1: Inversion

page 21

Task 1

1. D
2. C
3. B
4. A
5. F
6. E

Task 2

1. Hardly had we finished our meal when the phone started ringing.
2. No sooner had Mrs Thompson left one meeting than she had to go to another.
3. Only then did we realize what we had done.
4. Seldom have I met such an unpleasant person.

Station 2: Position of prepositions

page 22

Task

1. The atlas is on the third shelf of the bookcase in my room.
2. Sydney is on the south-east coast and it's the capital of New South Wales.
3. Your train will arrive at platform eight in five minutes and will leave at 8.55.
4. I often play darts with my friends. We go to a local pub near my home.
5. We often go to Italy for a short holiday at Christmas.
6. Sandra was born at 6 a.m. on 21st October in 1996.
7. Jim has lived in New York since 1999.
8. We had to wait for half an hour until the post office opened.

Station 3: Prepositions in relative clauses

page 23

Task

1. This isn't something we can agree to.
2. This is the street my grandparents used to live in.
3. Is this a lie you want to live with?
4. Do you know the names of all the stations we pass through?
5. I can't remember the name of the person I was talking to.
6. This elderly lady was the young girl I used to play with.
7. My parents still have the bike I learned to ride on.
8. Is this the young girl we were talking about?
9. The police searched for the book he had hidden the money in.
10. We looked for something we could start a fire with.

Station 4: *If, when* or *unless?*

page 24

Task

1. A Mr James might call and if he does, make an appointment for next Thursday.
2. I'm expecting an important fax from a client. Please bring it to me when it arrives.
3. I'm having a meeting, so don't put through any calls unless they're very important.
4. We'll take a taxi from the airport when we arrive.
5. We'll only take a taxi from the airport if we're short of time.
6. We won't take a taxi from the airport unless we're short of time.
7. She'll call us when she arrives at her hotel.
8. He won't call us unless something goes wrong.
9. We won't buy anything from your firm if you can't deliver on time.
10. We won't buy anything from your firm unless you deliver on time.
11. We'll pay your invoice when our branch office confirms delivery.

Station 5: Contact clauses

page 25

Task 1 and 2

1. The people ~~that~~ I work with aren't very friendly.
3. Does the train ~~that~~ you come to work on stop in Shoreditch?
5. 'Guernica' is one of the most famous pictures ~~which~~ Picasso painted at this time.
6. This is a photo ~~which~~ I took on my business trip to Dundee.
7. The quiz show ~~that~~ we watch usually asks some very difficult questions.
8. Someone stole the bike ~~that~~ I left outside the fitness studio.
11. The word processor ~~which~~ I use was designed in the USA.
12. Yes, that's the blue van ~~that~~ I saw parked in front of the bank.
13. What have you done with all the money ~~which~~ your grandparents gave you?
14. The last book ~~that~~ she wrote wasn't as successful as her previous ones.

Station 6: Passive in reported speech

page 26

Task

1. I was told (that) my report was to be written by the following Tuesday.
2. I was told (that) our office phone numbers were to be changed the following / next day.
3. I was told (that) my car could be repaired by the following Friday.
4. I was asked when the bill had to be paid.
5. I was told (that) I was to be given a better job.
6. I was told (that) my work had to be corrected far too often.
7. I was told (that) these orders had to be entered into the computer.
8. I was told (that) everything had had to be checked twice.
9. I was told (that) the post had been delivered an hour before.
10. I was told (that) Jane had had a little accident.

Station 7: Personal passive and impersonal passive

page 27

Task 1

1. I was offered a better job.
2. We've been given tickets for the football match.
3. You had been promised $100.
4. They'll quickly be shown the door.

Task 2

1. a) The girls were offered a lift into town.
   b) A lift into town was offered to the girls.
2. a) Everybody was given a prize.
   b) A prize was given to everybody.
3. a) The visitors were shown a film.
   b) A film was shown to the visitors.

Station 1: Simple past, past progressive and present perfect

page 28

Task

	Infinitiv	Simple Past	Present Perfect has/have …	Past Progressive was/were …
2.	*laufen*	ran	run	running
3.	*sitzen*	sat	sat	sitting
4.	*machen*	made	made	making
5.	*(mit)nehmen*	took	taken	taking
6.	*(aus)graben*	dug	dug	digging
7.	*anzünden*	lit	lit	lighting
8.	*sinken; versenken*	sank	sunk	sinking
9.	*denken; meinen*	thought	thought	thinking
10.	*werfen*	threw	thrown	throwing
11.	*füttern*	fed	fed	feeding
12.	*fangen*	caught	caught	catching
13.	*stehlen*	stole	stolen	stealing
14.	*verlieren*	lost	lost	losing
15.	*bezahlen*	paid	paid	paying
16.	*(aus)wählen*	chose	chosen	choosing
17.	*reiten, Rad fahren*	rode	ridden	riding
18.	*lehren; unterrichten*	taught	taught	teaching
19.	*wachsen; anbauen*	grew	grown	growing
20.	*(sich) treffen*	met	met	meeting

Station 2: Mixed past tenses (1)

page 29

Task 1 and 2

1. have often visited
2. have been taking
3. have toured
4. had never stayed
5. spent
6. didn't stay
7. chose
8. hired
9. drove
10. were looking for
11. had both retired
12. had been living
13. decided
14. was
15. found
16. had been looking for
17. bought
18. have modernized

Station 3: Mixed past tenses (2)

page 30

Task 1

NO.	Simple Past	Past Progressive	Present Perfect	Present Perfect Progressive	Past Perfect	Past Perfect Progressive
1.			✓			
2.				✓		
3.			✓			
4.					✓	
5.	✓					
6.	✓					
7.	✓					
8.	✓					
9.	✓					
10.		✓				
11.					✓	
12.						✓
13.	✓					
14.	✓					
15.	✓					
16.						✓
17.	✓					
18.			✓			

Task 2

1. How long have the Dillons been taking their holidays in Europe?
2. Which (European) countries have they toured?
3. Where did they spend their holidays last summer?
4. What were they looking for?
5. Where had they been living in Detroit?

Station 4: Future with *will/going to*

page 31

Task

1. I'll give
2. he's going to give
3. I'll show
4. I'll turn
5. I'm going to turn
6. Will you help
7. Are you going to help
8. I'll bring back
9. is finally going to buy
10. I'll call
11. I'm going to call

Station 5: Other future forms

page 32

Task

1. I expect to see him soon.
2. We want to buy a new car next week.
3. You are to report to Mr Madsen in one hour.
4. The president is to make a speech on television this evening.
5. I hope to go fishing tomorrow.
6. The King is to open the trade fair tomorrow.

Station 6: Mixed future tenses

page 33

Task 1

1. F
2. D
3. A
4. G
5. E
6. C
7. B

Task 2

1. will have finished
2. will have talked to
3. will have heard
4. won't have started
5. won't have left
6. won't have read
7. Will they have finished
8. Will the police have found
9. will have had

Station 7: Past participles (1)

page 34

Task

Across

3. bitten
5. become
6. fallen
7. drawn
9. begun
10. felt
11. brought
14. flown
15. cost
16. driven
18. forgotten
19. bought
20. done

Down

1. cut
2. frozen
3. bet
4. eaten
5. beaten
7. dreamt
8. found
9. broken
11. built
12. fought
13. drunk
17. come

Station 8: Past participles (2)

page 35

Task 1 and 2

1. get – got
2. give – given
3. go – gone
4. hang – hung
5. have – had
6. hear – heard
7. hide – hidden
8. hit – hit
9. hold – held
10. hurt – hurt
11. keep – kept
12. know – known
13. lead – led
14. learn – learnt
15. leave – left
16. lend – lent
17. let – let
18. put – put
19. read – read
20. ring – rung
21. say – said
22. see – seen

Station 9: The passive with different tenses

page 36

Task

1. D
2. E
3. C
4. B
5. G
6. F
7. A
8. J
9. E
10. G
11. H
12. I

Station 1: Uncountable nouns

page 37

Task 1

1. beer, lemonade
2. soup, tuna fish
3. coffee, mustard
4. butter, mincemeat
5. cake, cheese, bread, bacon
6. information, news
7. sauce, vinegar, milk, beer
8. tea, coffee, milk
9. jeans, trousers, pyjamas
10. bacon, sugar, cheese, tea, coffee
11. chocolate, soap
12. milk, sugar, cream, sauce, soup, yoghurt
13. cream, yoghurt, milk
14. chocolates

Task 2

1. I love chocolate.
2. I prefer chocolates.
3. The police are here.
4. I need more information.

Station 2: Conjunctions

page 38

Task 1

1. Although
2. because
3. after
4. because of
5. as if
6. that
7. If
8. (in order) to

Task 2

1. after
3. and
4. as
5. as well as
6. because
7. both … and
8. because of
9. but
10. if
12. even if
14. unless

Solutions: Tenses

Solutions: Revision

Station 3: *To* + infinitive

page 39

Task

Z	F	H	U	M	G	N	N	U	C	B	N	T	E	T
I	A	I	W	C	P	M	P	F	P	X	O	Y	E	A
P	K	R	N	Q	V	B	K	L	L	F	Y	W	J	N
Y	H	D	M	I	O	M	B	E	A	I	I	M	N	G
R	E	W	E	Y	S	L	H	R	Y	N	W	K	E	W
B	V	E	F	W	J	H	A	R	B	D	A	N	G	T
L	S	A	X	A	Q	L	A	T	U	W	J	P	F	B
Y	T	I	Y	D	N	E	Q	O	D	O	P	C	O	U
P	T	S	U	M	W	S	V	N	S	G	Q	R	R	S
D	Y	I	H	K	Q	A	W	Q	A	W	Z	O	D	G
E	Z	P	R	V	V	D	R	E	S	H	I	E	M	F
L	L	M	E	D	T	M	V	W	R	O	E	M	A	W
C	A	B	A	V	J	W	G	B	X	W	L	Q	K	B
K	Q	G	D	S	M	E	E	T	P	I	R	V	E	T
I	L	W	V	F	X	L	Y	O	K	U	Q	Y	E	G

1. to finish
2. to see
3. to read
4. to find
5. to be
6. to solve
7. to wear
8. to make
9. to play
10. to meet
11. to answer

Station 4: Infinitive with or without *to*

page 40

Task

1. crawl
2. to crawl
3. to buy
4. to buy
5. need
6. need to
7. to check
8. check
9. to dance, dance
10. to watch
11. watch
12. do
13. to do
14. (to) stand up
15. bury
16. to bury
17. to make
18. make
19. listen to
20. to listen to

Station 5: Position of prepositions

page 41

Task

1. Let's meet in front of the station at 3:30 on Saturday afternoon.
2. On Wednesday I went to the bank during my lunch break.
3. I sometimes go shopping at the weekend.
4. The swimming pool is always open from May to September.
5. I often hang out with my friends after school.
6. Dad and his friends have been playing poker for twelve years.
7. The opera is never over until the tall lady sings.
8. The library is opposite the town hall in the city centre.
9. We've been sitting here since 9:15 this morning!
10. I usually read a book before I go to bed.

Station 6: Simple past, past progressive and present perfect

page 42

Task 1

1. felt, arrived
2. was sitting, started
3. were walking, happened
4. woke up, was, was raining
5. heard, opened, ran out
6. were having, (were) watching, called

Task 2

1. I've never driven a car.
2. Did you visit Rome when you were in Italy last summer?
3. I've just bought a moped.
4. Have you found your coat yet?
5. Did anybody meet Mrs Bell at her hotel this morning?

Station 7: Mixed past tenses (1)

page 43

Task 1

1. bought
2. hasn't sold
3. has lent
4. passed
5. had had
6. sat
7. failed
8. thought
9. hadn't been looking
10. must have been
11. has been driving
12. hasn't had
13. has had
14. was

Task 2

1. Have you talked to
2. had
3. have decided
4. told
5. have found
6. Have you printed
7. has crashed
8. have been having

Station 8: Mixed past tenses (2)

page 44

Task

1. had been walking
2. found
3. had heard
4. (had) left
5. had made
6. had flown
7. saw
8. had been eating
9. waved
10. held
11. examined
12. switched off
13. haven't been able to
14. did
15. has been watching
16. left
17. knew
18. searched
19. threw
20. caught
21. was

Station 9: Future with *will/going to*

page 45

Task

1. The boy is soon going to fall off his bike. *(= kausale Schlussfolgerung)*
2. Be careful or you'll hurt yourself. *(= spontane Äußerung)*
3. It'll be dark in an hour./It's going to be dark in an hour.
4. I'm sure (that) Tom will be there. *(= Vermutung)*
5. It'll snow tomorrow./It's going to snow tomorrow.
6. We'll be very busy tomorrow./We're going to be very busy tomorrow.
7. I'm hungry, so I'll make a big sandwich. *(= spontane Entscheidung)*
8. Jane is going to buy the food for our party. *(= festes Vorhaben/Abmachung)*
9. We'll stop at the next filling station./We're going to stop at the next filling station.
10. I'm sure (that) Mark will like this CD. *(= Vermutung)*

Station 10: Mixed future tenses

page 46

Task

1. I'm studying / I'll be studying
2. will go
3. it's going to stop
4. will have been working
5. will you be doing
6. will we stay / are we going to stay
7. I'll tidy it up
8. will have finished
9. will have eaten
10. she's going to help
11. will you talk about / will you be talking about

Station 11: Past participles

page 47

Task 1 + 2

1. seek – sought
2. sell – sold
3. send – sent
4. shake – shaken
5. shine – shone
6. shoot – shot
7. show – shown
8. shut – shut
9. sing – sung
10. sleep – slept
11. speak – spoken
12. spend – spent
13. spread – spread
14. stand – stood
15. stick – stuck
16. swear – sworn
17. sweep – swept
18. swing – swung
19. tear – torn
20. understand – understood
21. wake – woken
22. wear – worn
23. win – won
24. write – written

Station 12: Reported speech and passive

page 48

Task 1

1. Tom said (that) our next game would be played on the computer.
2. Detective Wright said (that) everybody in the building had been interviewed.
3. Mr Hall said (that) it was cold and asked if we all had been given extra blankets.
4. Susan told us (that) she had heard the news and wanted to know if / whether the thieves had been caught.
5. Wendy told us to stop the game before somebody got hurt.

Task 2

1. Mr Hirohito will be met at the airport. / Mr Hirohito is to be met at the airport.
2. A taxi has been ordered for Mr Wells.
3. Nests / Birds' nests are usually built in the spring.
4. Have your parents been informed about the class trip?
5. I'm thought to be very strange.
6. Where can Mr Simpson be found?

Transcripts of the listening comprehension texts

Track 1 – Station 3: Uncountable nouns (1), Task 2 (Basics, S. 11)

Mrs Gibbons had invited some colleagues from her firm to a party. There was plenty of music, food and drinks. Dan had a good time. He danced with two pretty girls and drank lots of mineral water. He ate a few sandwiches and lots of crisps and peanuts. Later he had a big glass of red wine and a little cheese with bread and some smoked fish. Then he discovered the giant tomatoes! They were filled with a delicious cream. There were three of these filled tomatoes on the table and Dan ate all three! At the end of the party Dan told Mrs Gibbons that he had enjoyed everything. Mrs Gibbons said rather sharply, "Yes, I noticed. You even ate the cips!"

Track 2 – Station 10: Relative Pronouns, Task 1 (Basics, S. 18)

BLARNEY, which has versions for both Windows and Macintosh, is a complete text-processing and layout program. It contains formatting options which can be used by both amateur and professional users. It provides all the features that experienced users now expect from a competent word processor. There are pull-down menus that offer easy-to-use options. There is a built-in universal converter which can open any document whatever the program that created it. The well-organized printed handbook is also available on-screen, which saves time. Users who register their software with us will be offered a fifty per cent reduction on all future updates. A free download service is also available to all users whose registration number is known to us.

Track 3 – Station 11: *To* + infinitive, Task 2 (Basics, S. 19)

I'll never forget Whitley Bay. My parents used to take me there for a holiday in the summer. We would spend one or even two weeks at a drab boarding house in a side street far from the beach. In those days they couldn't afford to stay anywhere else.

I'll never forget the name of the landlady, Mrs Thistlethwaite, because as a child I found it difficult to pronounce her name without spitting on the floor. She was a grim woman. Breakfast was at exactly eight o'clock and none of her guests dared to be either too early or too late. She expected her guests, whatever their age, to behave themselves and do exactly what she told them to do. Children had to be especially clean and quiet – in other words: invisible. She never forgot to remind us not to play on the stairs or in the labyrinthine corridors of her Victorian residence. There were usually several young children and she watched us constantly. We knew she was just waiting for us to do something wrong and then she would complain to our parents.

Mrs Thistlethwaite made all her guests leave the boarding house by nine o'clock so that their rooms could be cleaned. And she let nobody return until tea-time at five o'clock. And so after a breakfast of weak tea and thin slices of bread and margarine with jam it was time for us to enjoy the attractions of Whitley Bay: seaside shops selling candy floss, rock and fish and chips, an amusement park called 'Fun City' and, ultimately, the sea beyond a long sandy beach. I can remember all these things with pleasure.

But rainy days in Whitley Bay were hell. You couldn't sit on the beach for hours in the rain and an icy wind. The cinemas didn't open until the evening and after an hour or so even 'Fun City' failed to appeal. I can remember sitting in spartan cafés – they were all the same: uncomfortable chairs and formica table-tops with overflowing ashtrays and puddles of spilled tea or coffee – and trying to make a small glass of orange juice last an hour.

I'd love to return to Whitley Bay, but when I do, it will be on a fine sunny day and I'll keep well away from those gloomy boarding houses of my childhood!

Track – Station 5: Contact clauses, Task 2 (The sentence, S. 25)

Number 1: The people I work with aren't very friendly.
Number 3: Does the train you come to work on stop in Shoreditch?
Number 5: 'Guernica' is one of the most famous pictures Picasso painted at this time.
Number 6: This is a photo I took on my business trip to Dundee.
Number 7: The quiz show we watch usually asks some very difficult questions.
Number 8: Someone stole the bike I left outside the fitness studio.
Number 11: The word processor I use was designed in the USA.
Number 12: Yes, that's the blue van I saw parked in front of the bank.
Number 13: What have you done with all the money your grandparents gave you?
Number 14: The last book she wrote wasn't as successful as her previous ones.

Track 1 – Station 2: Mixed past tenses (1), Task 2 (Tenses, S. 29)

Dr Dillon and his wife have often visited Europe. They have been taking their holidays in Europe for fifteen years now. In all this time they've toured several countries: Britain, France, Italy, Spain, Germany and Austria. But until last year they had never stayed in any country longer than a couple of days.

Last summer they spent their entire summer holiday in Britain. And they didn't stay in London this time, either. They chose a comfortable hotel in Dover, hired a car and drove along the south coast of England. They were looking for a typical English cottage in a quiet, peaceful village. The Dillons had both retired at the beginning of that year. They had been living in a city-centre apartment in Detroit for over thirty years. They decided that it was time for a change. They finally found the place they had been looking for in a little village called Polperro. They bought an old fisherman's cottage there which they have now extended and modernized.

Track 2 – Station 8: Past participles (2), Task 1 (Tenses, S. 35)

Number 1: get
Number 2: give
Number 3: go
Number 4: hang
Number 5: have
Number 6: hear
Number 7: hide
Number 8: hit
Number 9: hold
Number 10: hurt
Number 11: keep
Number 12: know
Number 13: lead
Number 14: learn
Number 15: leave
Number 16: lend
Number 17: let
Number 18: put
Number 19: read
Number 20: ring
Number 21: say
Number 22: see

Track 1 – Station 2: Conjunctions, Task 2 (Revision, S. 38)

Tom and Mary often arrive at the sports club together. Both he and Mary work for the same firm, but not in the same department. They're friends as well as colleagues. As they live near each other, they often share a car. They usually go for a drink after they leave the sports club. They always stop at the King's Head because it's on their way home. They like that pub because of its friendly atmosphere. Mary likes a gin tonic unless she's driving. If she's driving, she drinks mineral water. Tom never drinks alcohol even if Mary is driving.

Track 2 – Station 7: Mixed past tenses (1), Task 1 (Revision, S. 43)

Christine bought a new car last month, but she hasn't sold her old car yet. She has lent her old car to her younger brother Danny for a year. He finally passed his driving test last week. He had had almost forty driving lessons before he sat the test. He failed his first driving test because the examiner thought he hadn't been looking in the mirror often enough. That must have been sometime last April. Christine has been driving for six years now and she hasn't had any serious accidents. She has had her own car since she was nineteen

Track 3 – Station 11: Past participles, Task 1 (Revision, S. 47)

Number 1: seek
Number 2: sell
Number 3: send
Number 4: shake
Number 5: shine
Number 6: shoot
Number 7: show
Number 8: shut
Number 9: sing
Number 10: sleep
Number 11: speak
Number 12: spend
Number 13: spread
Number 14: stand
Number 15: stick
Number 16: swear
Number 17: sweep
Number 18: swing
Number 19: tear
Number 20: understand
Number 21: wake
Number 22: wear
Number 23: win
Number 24: write